Mathematics

THE STORY OF NUMBERS, SYMBOLS, AND SPACE

by IRVING ADLER

Illustrated by LOWELL HESS

j 510

GOLDEN PRESS 🦅 NEW YORK

Library of Congress Catalog Card Number 61-5441

Fourth Printing, 1962

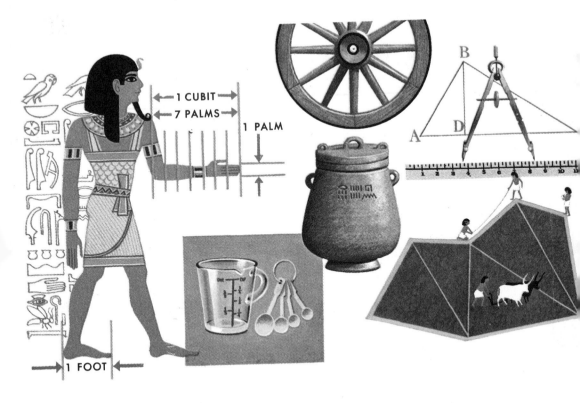

What Is Mathematics?

Mathematics is the science in which we think carefully about numbers and space. It helps us keep score at a baseball game, measure the area of a floor, figure out our income tax, or decide which article is a better buy. It helps the engineer design a machine. At work or at play, we often have to answer questions like, "How many?", "How big?", or "How far?" To answer such questions we have to use numbers. We have to know how numbers are related to each other, and how different parts of space fit together. To be sure our answers are correct, we try to think carefully. When we do these things, we are using mathematics.

In the days when men got their food by hunting and by gathering wild fruits and berries, they had to count to keep track of their supplies. Counting, measuring, and calculating became even more important when people became farmers and shepherds. They had to measure land and count their flocks. When they built irrigation dams and canals, they had to figure out how much earth to remove, and how many stones

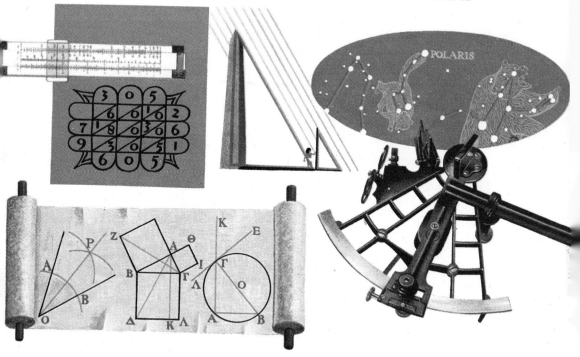

Ancient merchants, builders, and navigators all used mathematics to solve their problems.

and bricks they would use. The overseers had to know in advance, too, how much food to store up for the force of working men.

Carpenters and masons had to measure and calculate as they built homes for the people, palaces for their rulers, and great tombs like the pyramids for their dead kings.

As trade flourished, merchants measured and weighed their wares, put a proper price on them, figured their costs and their profits, and counted their money.

Tax collectors figured the tax rate, and kept accounts. To deal with all these activities, men invented *arithmetic*, which studies numbers, and *geometry*, which studies space.

To predict the changes of the seasons, priests studied the motions of the sun, moon, and stars. Navigators looked to the sky, too, for the stars that guided them from place to place. To help them in this work, men invented *trigonometry*, the branch of mathematics that relates distances to directions.

Commerce spread over the world. The same kinds of calculations often had to be repeated. To save time, some people worked out rules for doing them, and ways of doing many problems all at once. This was the beginning of the branch of mathematics called *algebra*.

7

Written Numbers

Men have used written numbers for about seven thousand years. As time passed, they invented new and better ways of writing them. At first they wrote numbers by making notches in a stick, or lines on the ground. We still use this system when we write the Roman numerals I, II, and III. We find it hidden, too, in our Arabic numerals 2 and 3. They began as sets of

	1	2	3	4	5	6	7	8	9	10	100	
EGYPTIAN	I	II	III	IIII	III II	III III	IIII III	IIII IIII	III III III	∩	℮	
BABYLONIAN	Y	YY	YYY	YYYY	YYY YY	YYY YYY	YYYY YYY	YYYY YYYY	YYYY YYYY YYY	⟨		
EARLY ROMAN	I	II	III	IIII	V	VI	VII	VIII	IX	X	C	C
CHINESE	一	二	三	四	五	六	七	八	九	十	百	
HINDU	?	?	?	?	?	?	?	?	?	?		
MAYAN	•	••	•••	••••	—	•̄	••̄	•••̄	••••̄	=	⬭	

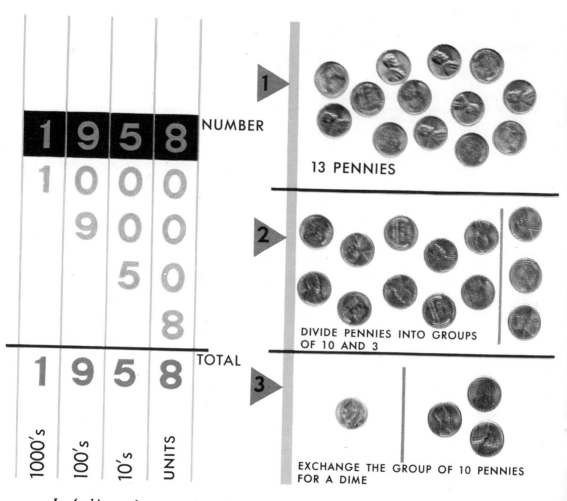

1000's	100's	10's	UNITS	
1	**9**	**5**	**8**	NUMBER
1	0	0	0	
	9	0	0	
		5	0	
			8	
1	**9**	**5**	**8**	TOTAL

1 ▸ 13 PENNIES

2 ▸ DIVIDE PENNIES INTO GROUPS OF 10 AND 3

3 ▸ EXCHANGE THE GROUP OF 10 PENNIES FOR A DIME

In Arabic numbers over nine, the value of each digit depends on its position.

separated strokes. Then, when the strokes were written in a hurry, they were joined to each other.

The Arabic numbers use only ten symbols, the digits 0, 1, 2, 3, 4, 5, 6, 7, 8, 9. But with these ten digits, we can write down any number we like. We do this by breaking large numbers into groups, just as we do with money. We can separate thirteen pennies into groups of ten and three. We can ex-change the ten pennies for a dime. Then we have *one* dime and *three* pennies. To write the number thirteen, we write 13. The 1 written in the second space from the right means one group of ten, just as one dime means one group of ten pennies.

In the same way, a number written in the third space from the right means groups of hundreds, in the fourth space, thousands, and so on.

9

2357 Numbers We Cannot Split

You can make a "picture" of a whole number by using a line of checkers. To form the picture, use as many checkers as the number tells you to.

A line of four checkers can be split into two lines with two checkers each. If we put these lines under each other, the checkers form a rectangle. Rectangles can also be formed with 6, 8, 9, or 10 checkers. So we call these numbers *rectangle numbers*. The rectangle for the number 10 has 2 lines that have 5 checkers in each line. Notice that $2 \times 5 = 10$. *Every rectangle number is the product of smaller numbers.*

There are some numbers that cannot be split in this way. For example, we cannot arrange 7 checkers in a rectangle. We can arrange them in seven lines, with one checker in each line. But then they are still arranged in a single line, only now the line runs up and down, instead of going from right to left. The number 7 is not a rectangle number. Numbers that cannot be pictured as a rectangle are called *prime* numbers. They cannot be written as the product of smaller numbers.

There is a simple way of finding out whether a number is a rectangle number or a prime number. This method is called the sieve of Eratosthenes, after the Greek scientist who devised the system, two centuries before the birth of Christ. Imagine all the whole numbers, starting with 2, arranged in order in a line. The number 2, which stands at the head of the line, is a prime number. Now count by 2's, and cross out every number you get. This removes the number 2, and all multiples of 2. They are numbers like 4, 6, 8, and so on, that form rectangles with two lines. Among the numbers that are left, the

A rectangle number is always the product of smaller numbers.

RECTANGLE NUMBERS

	2	3	4	5	6	7	8	9	10	11	12	13	14	15	16	17
COUNT OFF BY 2's	2	3	4	5	6	7	8	9	10	11	12	13	14	15	16	17
COUNT OFF BY 3's		3		5		7		9		11		13		15		17
COUNT OFF BY 5's				5		7				11		13				17
COUNT OFF BY 7's						7				11		13				17

The sieve of Eratosthenes is a method of finding prime numbers.

number 3 now stands at the head of the line. It is the next prime number. Now cross out the numbers you get when you count by 3's. This removes the number 3, and all multiples of 3. They are numbers like 9 and 15, that form rectangles with three lines. Number 5 now stands at the head of the line. It is the third prime number. Continue in this way, removing from the line the number at the head of the line, and all multiples of that number. After each family of numbers is removed, the number that stands at the head of the line is the next prime number.

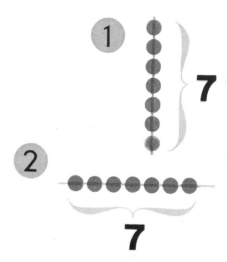

Prime numbers cannot be written as the product of smaller numbers.

The Shapes of Numbers

Numbers, like people, come in many shapes. Some numbers form rectangles and some do not. There are also some numbers that form triangles, or squares, or cubes.

TRIANGLE NUMBERS

We find the numbers that form triangles by placing lines of checkers under each other. Put 1 checker in the first line, 2 checkers in the second line, 3 in the third line, and so on. The total number is called a triangle number. The first four triangle numbers are 1, 3, 6, and 10. What is the seventh triangle number? One way to find out is to make the seventh triangle. Then count the number of checkers in it. But there is a short cut we can use. The drawing (p. 13), shows the seventh tri-

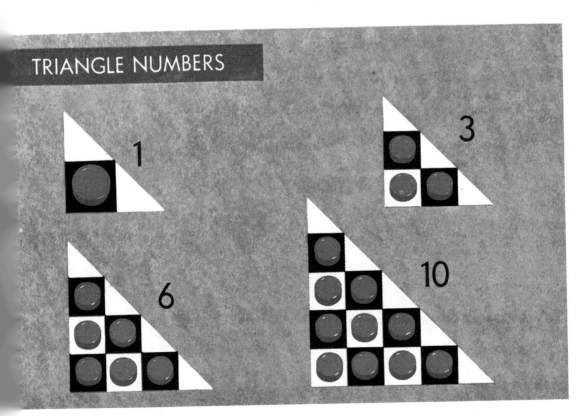

TRIANGLE NUMBERS

1

3

6

10

angle, with another one just like it placed next to it upside down. The two triangles together form a rectangle, so the triangle number is half of the rectangle number. The rectangle has seven lines, and eight checkers in each line. So the rectangle number is 7 × 8, or 56. Half of that is 28. To find a triangle number, multiply the number of lines in the triangle by the next higher number and then take half of the product. To find the eighth triangle number, take half of 8 × 9.

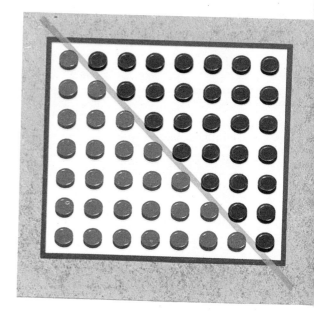

SQUARE NUMBERS

We form a square by making a rectangle in which the number of lines is the same as the number of checkers in each line. The smallest square has only one line, with one checker in the line. So the smallest square number is 1. The next square has two lines, with two checkers in each line. So the second square number is 2 × 2, or 4. The third square number is 3 × 3, or 9. To get a square number, multiply any number by itself. The seventh square number is 7 × 7, or 49. We call it "seven squared," and sometimes write it as 7^2. The little 2 written in the upper right hand corner is just a way of showing that the 7 is to be used as a multiplier twice.

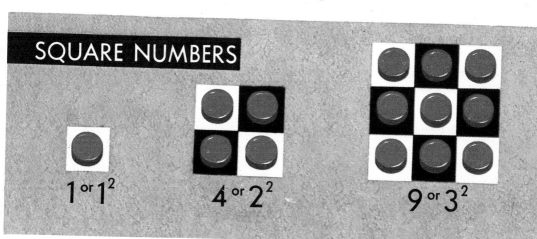

SQUARE NUMBERS

1 or 1^2 4 or 2^2 9 or 3^2

	1	2	3	4	5	6	7	8	9	10
1	1	2	3	4	5	6	7	8	9	10
2	2	4	6	8	10	12	14	16	18	20
3	3	6	9	12	15	18	21	24	27	30
4	4	8	12	16	20	24	28	32	36	40
5	5	10	15	20	25	30	35	40	45	50
6	6	12	18	24	30	36	42	48	54	60
7	7	14	21	28	35	42	49	56	63	70
8	8	16	24	32	40	48	56	64	72	80
9	9	18	27	36	45	54	63	72	81	90
10	10	20	30	40	50	60	70	80	90	100

The square numbers are relatives of the odd numbers (numbers that cannot form rectangles with two lines). If you list the odd numbers in order, stop when you like and add those you have listed, the sum is always a square number. The drawing below shows you why this is so.

The square numbers are also relatives of the triangle numbers. Add any triangle number to the next higher triangle number, and you always get a square number.

CUBIC NUMBERS

If we use blocks instead of checkers, we can arrange them in lines to form a square. Then, we can pile the squares on top of each other in layers. When the number of layers is equal to the

The sum of any consecutive series of odd numbers will always be a square number.

$$1 = 1^2$$
$$1 + 3 = 2^2 \text{ or } 4$$
$$1 + 3 + 5 = 3^2 \text{ or } 9$$
$$1 + 3 + 5 + 7 = 4^2 \text{ or } 16$$

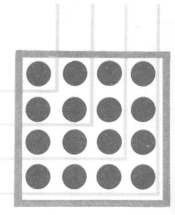

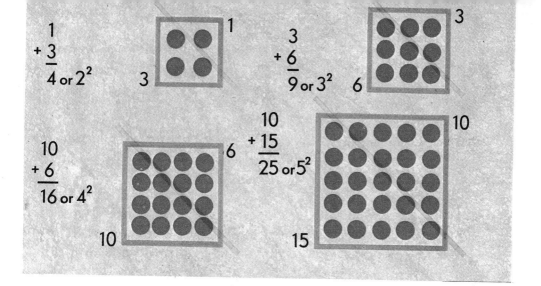

$$\begin{array}{r} 1 \\ +3 \\ \hline 4 \text{ or } 2^2 \end{array}$$

3

1

$$\begin{array}{r} 3 \\ +6 \\ \hline 9 \text{ or } 3^2 \end{array}$$

6

3

$$\begin{array}{r} 10 \\ +6 \\ \hline 16 \text{ or } 4^2 \end{array}$$

10

6

$$\begin{array}{r} 10 \\ +15 \\ \hline 25 \text{ or } 5^2 \end{array}$$

10

15

number of blocks in a line, we have a cube. The number of blocks in a cube is called a cubic number. The smallest cubic number is 1. The second cubic number is $2 \times 2 \times 2$, or 8. We call it "two cubed," and sometimes write it as 2^3. The little 3 written in the upper right hand corner shows that the 2 is to be used as a multiplier three times. The fifth cubic number is "five cubed." It is written as 5^3, and means $5 \times 5 \times 5$, or 125.

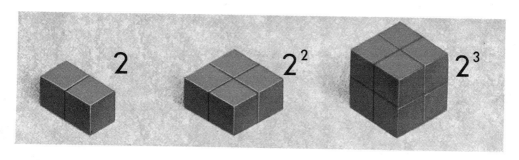

2   2^2 2^3

1^3 2^3 3^3 4^3

Rabbits and Plants

A man bought a pair of rabbits and bred them. The pair produced one pair of young after one month, and a second pair after the second month. Then they stopped breeding. Each new pair also produced two more pairs in the same way, and then stopped breeding. How many new pairs of rabbits did he get each month?

To answer this question, let us write down in a line the number of pairs in each generation. First write the number 1 for the single pair he started with.

Next we write the number 1 for the pair they produced after a month.

The next month both pairs had young, so the next number is 2. We now have three numbers in a line: 1, 1, 2. Each number represents a new generation. Now the first generation stopped producing. The second generation (1 pair) produced 1 pair. The third generation (2 pairs) produced 2 pairs. So the next number we write is $1 + 2$, or 3. Now the second generation stopped producing. The third generation (2 pairs) produced 2 pairs. The fourth generation (3 pairs) produced 3 pairs. So the next number we write is $2 + 3$, or 5.

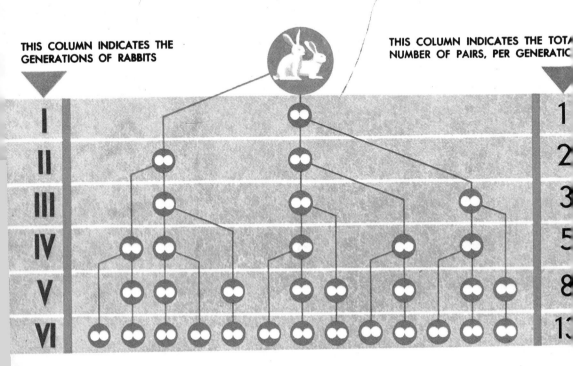

THIS COLUMN INDICATES THE
GENERATIONS OF RABBITS

THIS COLUMN INDICATES THE TOTAL
NUMBER OF PAIRS, PER GENERATION

I	1
II	2
III	3
IV	5
V	8
VI	13

Each month, only the last two generations produced, so we can get the next number by adding the last two two numbers in the line. The numbers we get in this way are called *Fibonacci numbers*. The first twelve of them are: 1, 1, 2, 3, 5, 8, 13, 21, 34, 55, 89, 144. They have interesting properties and keep popping up in many places in nature.

Here is one of the properties of these numbers. Pick any three numbers that follow each other in the line. Multiply the middle number by itself, and the first number by the third number. The results will always differ by 1. For example, if we take the numbers 3, 5, 8, we get $5^2 = 5 \times 5 = 25$, while $3 \times 8 = 24$. If we take the numbers 5, 8, 13, we find that $8^2 = 64$, while $5 \times 13 = 65$.

Now take each number and divide it by its neighbor on the right. We get a series of fractions,

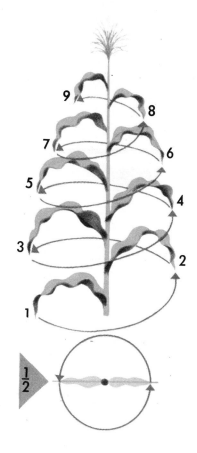

$$\frac{1}{1}, \frac{1}{2}, \frac{2}{3}, \frac{3}{5}, \frac{5}{8}, \frac{8}{13}, \frac{13}{21}, \frac{21}{34}, \frac{34}{55}, \frac{55}{89}, \frac{89}{144}$$

These fractions describe the growth of plants. When new leaves grow from the stem of a plant, they spiral around the stem. The spiral turns as it climbs. If the number of leaves in one turn is more than two but less than three, the leaves that are nearest each other line up in two sets of spirals around the stem. One set winds around and up to the right. The other set winds around and up to the left. If the number of

Fibonacci fractions have several interesting properties. One can be used to describe the spirals that are formed by plant leaves as they grow from the stem. The precise spacing of the ascending leaves allows sunlight to filter down to the lower leaves of the plant.

separate spirals that wind to the left is divided by the number of separate spirals that wind to the right, the result is a Fibonacci fraction. The Fibonacci fractions show up in the same way in the arrangement of the scales on a pine cone or the florets of a flower.

17

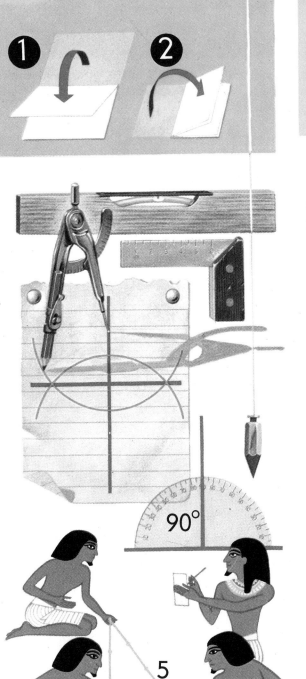

Right Angles

The angle that we use the most often is an angle of 90 degrees. We call it a right angle. We make bricks with right angles in each corner so they will stack up easily upon each other.

A bricklayer makes a right angle with strings. He makes one string horizontal with a level. He makes the other string exactly vertical by hanging a weight from its end. In this way, he makes a perfect right angle to guide him as he lays his bricks, so that the walls of his building will be straight and true.

In ancient Egypt, surveyors made a right angle by "rope-stretching." They used a long rope that was divided into twelve equal spaces by knots. One man held the two ends of the rope together. A second man held the knot that was three spaces from one end. A third man held the knot that was four spaces from the other end. Pulled tight, the rope formed a right angle.

The simplest way of making a right angle is to fold a piece of paper. Then fold it again so that the edges of the first crease line up exactly.

A right angle is an angle of 90 degrees. Early Egyptians formed a right angle by stretching an evenly knotted rope.

Triangles and the Distance to the Moon

Triangles may have different sizes and shapes, but the three angles of any triangle always add up to the same amount. To see this for yourself, cut a triangle out of paper. Then tear off the three angles. Place them side by side and corner to corner. You will see that they form two right angles, or exactly 180 degrees. This fact gives you a short cut for finding all the angles of any triangle, even if you measure only two of them. For example, if one of the angles is 40 degrees, and the second one is 60 degrees, you can find the number of degrees in the third angle without measuring it. Simply add 40 to 60 and subtract the result from 180.

The third angle will be 80 degrees.

This short cut is especially helpful if the third angle is out of reach. For example, suppose that two men, standing at separate places on the earth, look at the moon. The two men and the moon form a triangle. We can't measure the angle at the moon, but we can calculate it from the angles we can measure on earth.

Being able to calculate the angle at the moon is important to astronomers because it helps them to calculate the distance to the moon. If the moon were further away than it is, the angle would be smaller. If the moon were closer, the angle would be larger.

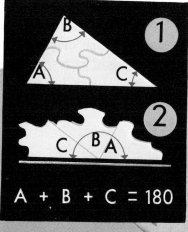

$$A + B + C = 180$$

No matter what size or shape they are, the number of degrees in the three angles of a triangle always add up to 180 degrees.

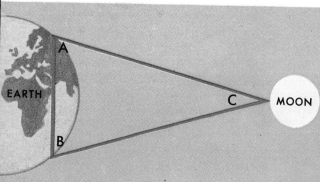

EARTH

MOON

Getting Through the Doorway

Sandy was building a large model airplane out in the little shed which was his workshop. As he was about to glue the wings to the body of the plane, Sandy thought, "I wonder if I'll be able to get the plane through the shed doorway after I put the wings on. The wingspread is 5½ feet across, and the shed doorway is 3 feet wide and 5 feet high."

Sandy couldn't get the plane through the doorway upright, but he might do it by tipping the wings to one side.

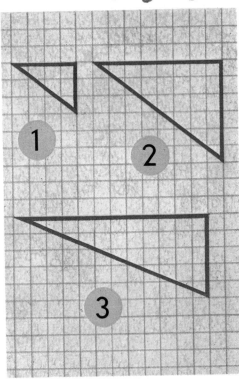

We can help Sandy solve his problem by finding out how the sides of a right triangle are related to each other. On a sheet of graph paper, make a right triangle 4 units wide (first leg) and 3 units high (second leg). Measure the hypotenuse (the longest side). It will be 5 units long. Now make two more right triangles, as in the diagram. Measure the hypotenuse of each triangle:

leg	leg	hypotenuse
4	3	5
8	6	10
12	5	13

Look at the numbers for each triangle. There doesn't seem to be any obvious connection between them. But there is a hidden connection. It shows itself when we square each number:

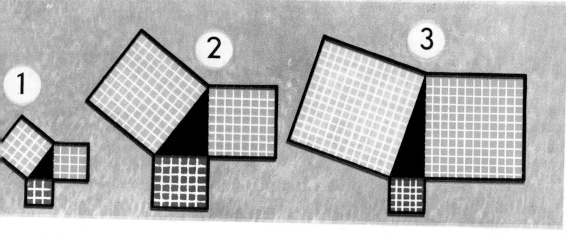

A rule discovered by Pythagoras over 2500 years ago states that the square of one leg plus the square of the second leg always equals the square of the hypotenuse, in a right triangle.

(first leg)^2	(second leg)^2	(hypotenuse)^2
$4 \times 4 = 16$	$3 \times 3 = 9$	$5 \times 5 = 25$, and $16 + 9 = 25$
$8 \times 8 = 64$	$6 \times 6 = 36$	$10 \times 10 = 100$ $64 + 36 = 100$
$12 \times 12 = 144$	$5 \times 5 = 25$	$13 \times 13 = 169$ $144 + 25 = 169$

These are examples of a rule discovered about 2500 years ago by a Greek mathematician named Pythagoras. The rule says that in every right triangle, the square of one leg plus the square of the other leg equals the square of the hypotenuse, or, $(\text{leg})^2 + (\text{leg})^2 = (\text{hypotenuse})^2$.

If we use this rule, it will help us to solve Sandy's problem. We can see that the width, the height, and the diagonal of the shed doorway form a right triangle. Its legs are 3 feet and 5 feet. $3^2 + 5^2 = 9 + 25 = 34$. Because 34 is the square of the diagonal through which the airplane must pass, we must square the wingspread of the plane, in order to see whether it is smaller than the diagonal of the doorway. The wingspread is 5½ feet.

$(5½)^2 = 5½ \times 5½ = \frac{11}{2} \times \frac{11}{2} = \frac{121}{4} = 30¼$

This result is less than 34, so, by tilting the plane on a diagonal, Sandy will be able to get it through the doorway.

Here are three sets of numbers. Two of the sets obey the rule of Pythagoras. Which ones are they?

9	12	15
8	15	17
12	15	18

The first two sets obey the rule.

21

Circles and Toothpicks

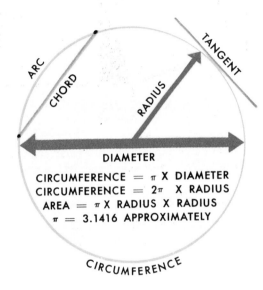

ARC
CHORD
RADIUS
DIAMETER
TANGENT
CIRCUMFERENCE

CIRCUMFERENCE = π X DIAMETER
CIRCUMFERENCE = 2π X RADIUS
AREA = π X RADIUS X RADIUS
π = 3.1416 APPROXIMATELY

We see circles everywhere. The wheels of automobiles, the rims of cups and saucers, and the faces of nickels and quarters are all circles. The sun and the full moon look like circles in the sky.

The distance across a circle, through its center, is called the *diameter* of the circle. The distance around the circle is called its *circumference*. Measure the diameter of a quarter, and you will find that it is about one inch long. You can measure the circumference of the quarter, too. First, wind enough string around it to go around once. Then unwind the string and measure it with a ruler. You will find that it is about three times as long as the diameter. The circumference of *any* circle is always the same number times the diameter. This number cannot be written exactly as a fraction or decimal, so we use a Greek letter, π (pi), to stand for it. It is almost equal to $3\frac{1}{7}$ or 3.14.

Strange as it may seem, there is an interesting way of calculating the value of π by dropping a stick on a floor. The

The circumference, or distance around any circle, always equals its diameter multiplied by 3.14, the number known as pi.

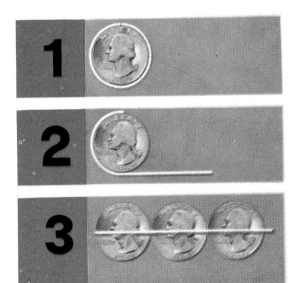

floor has to be made of planks of the same width. Use a thin stick that is as long as the planks are wide. A toothpick may be just right. Now, you simply drop the stick to the ground over and over. Count the number of times you drop it, and the number of times it falls on a crack between planks. Double the number of throws, and then divide by the number of times it fell on a crack. The result will be your value of π.

For example, if you drop the stick 100 times, and it falls on a crack only 62 times, divide 200 by 62. The result is a little more than 3.2 This is not a very accurate value of π. The more times you drop the stick, the more accurate a value you will get. When you drop the stick, whether or not it crosses a crack depends on where its center falls, and how it is turned around its center.

When a stick turns around its center, it moves around in a circle. That is why π, which is related to measuring a circle, is also related to the chance that the stick will cross a crack.

Another interesting way of calculating π uses the odd numbers, 1, 3, 5, 7, 9, and so on. First write the fractions, $\frac{1}{1}$ $\frac{1}{3}$ $\frac{1}{5}$ $\frac{1}{7}$ $\frac{1}{9}$ etc. Then, starting with the first fraction, subtract the second one, add the third one, subtract the fourth one, and so on. Stop whenever you like, and multiply by 4. The result will be a number close to π. The more fractions you use before you stop, the closer the value will be.

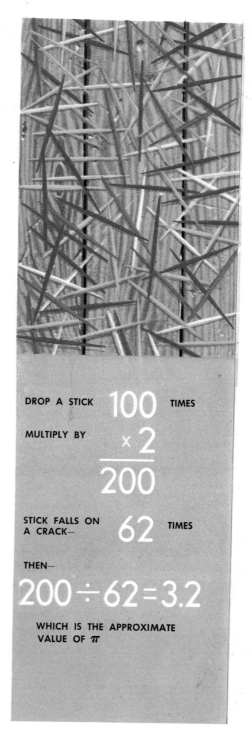

DROP A STICK **100** TIMES

MULTIPLY BY $\times 2$

200

STICK FALLS ON A CRACK— **62** TIMES

THEN—

$200 \div 62 = 3.2$

WHICH IS THE APPROXIMATE VALUE OF π

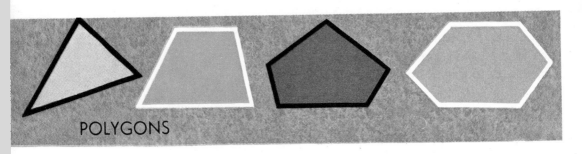

POLYGONS

Equal Sides and Equal Angles

A closed figure whose sides are straight is called a polygon. Triangles and squares are polygons. The number of angles in a polygon is the same as the number of sides.

Some polygons have equal sides and equal angles. They are *regular polygons*. A regular polygon may have any number of sides, starting with three. One way of making a regular polygon is to calculate the number of degrees each angle should have, and then make these angles with a protractor, separating them with equal sides. To get the num-

ber of degrees in the *sum* of the angles of any polygon, take two less than the number of sides, and multiply by 180. If the figure has three sides, the angles must add up to 180 degrees. (3 angles, minus 2 = 1. 1 × 180 = 180°.) So, for three equal angles, we divide the sum of the angles (180) by 3. This gives us the amount of each angle. Therefore, each of the three angles must be 60 degrees. If the figure has four sides, the angles add up to 360 degrees. (4 angles minus 2 = 2. 2 × 180 = 360.) So each of the four equal angles is 90 degrees.

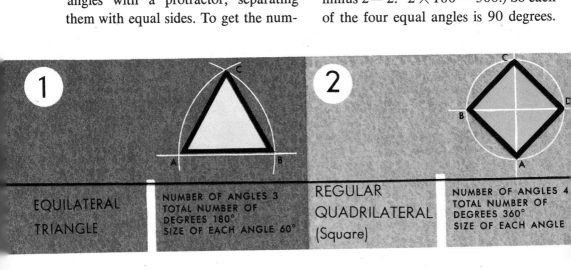

| EQUILATERAL TRIANGLE | NUMBER OF ANGLES 3 TOTAL NUMBER OF DEGREES 180° SIZE OF EACH ANGLE 60° | REGULAR QUADRILATERAL (Square) | NUMBER OF ANGLES 4 TOTAL NUMBER OF DEGREES 360° SIZE OF EACH ANGLE |

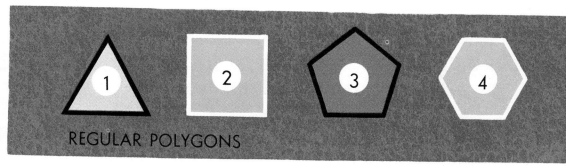

REGULAR POLYGONS

name	number of angles	sum of angles in degrees	size of each angle in degrees
1. equilateral triangle	3	180	60
2. square	4	360	90
3. regular pentagon	5	540	108
4. regular hexagon	6	720	120

You can make an equilateral triangle with a ruler and compasses by the method shown in the drawing. To make a square, first make a circle. Fold the paper so that the crease passes through the center of the circle. Now fold the paper again, to make a right angle at the center. Open up the paper, and join the points where the creases cross the circle. To make a regular pentagon, cut a long strip of paper of uniform width. Then tie it into a knot, as shown in the drawing, and press the knot flat. To make a regular hexagon, draw a circle, and then mark off pieces on the circle, with your compasses opened to the same width you used to make the circle. There will be exactly six equal pieces. Join the ends of each marked-off piece by a straight line to make the hexagon.

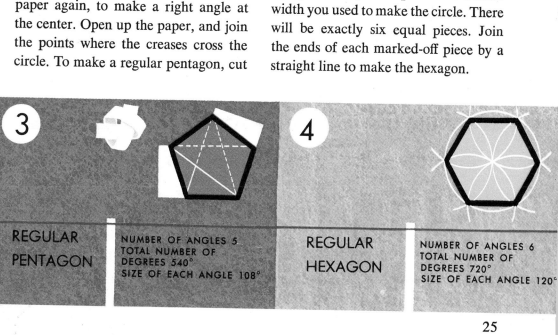

REGULAR PENTAGON

NUMBER OF ANGLES 5
TOTAL NUMBER OF DEGREES 540°
SIZE OF EACH ANGLE 108°

REGULAR HEXAGON

NUMBER OF ANGLES 6
TOTAL NUMBER OF DEGREES 720°
SIZE OF EACH ANGLE 120°

25

Salt and Diamonds

Many minerals form beautiful crystals with smooth flat faces and sharp edges. In some of these crystals, the faces are regular polygons that have the same size and shape, with the same number of polygons at each corner. A solid that is built in this way is called a *regular solid*.

There are exactly five regular solids. Their names show the number of faces that they have. The *tetrahedron* (four faces) is made of triangles, with three triangles at each corner. The *hexahedron* or cube (six faces) is made of squares, with three squares at each corner. The *octahedron* (eight faces) is made of triangles, with four triangles at each corner. The *dodecahedron* (twelve faces) is made of pentagons, with three pentagons at each corner. The *icosahe-*

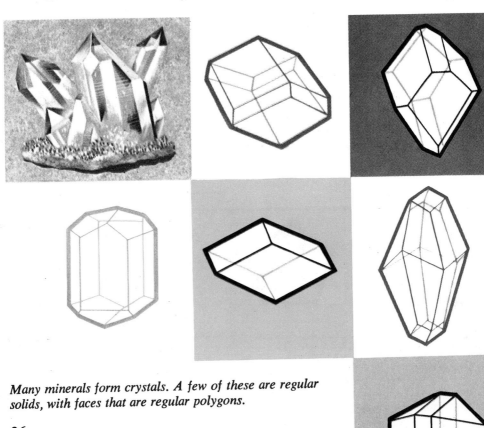

Many minerals form crystals. A few of these are regular solids, with faces that are regular polygons.

dron (twenty faces) is made of triangles, with five triangles at each corner.

An interesting characteristic of all solids with flat faces is that if you add all the corners to the number of faces of the solid, you will get the number of edges in the solid, plus 2. Try it with the cube shown in the picture on page 28. There are eight corners and six faces, which add up to 14. Now count the number of edges. There are 12 different edges.

If you look at table salt under a magnifying glass, you will see that each crystal is a cube. A diamond crystal is often an octahedron.

The regular solids make interesting decorations. Some are now made for sale as paperweights. There are calendars printed on a dodecahedron, with each month on a separate face. You can make a model for each of the regular solids by using the patterns shown here. First make an equilateral triangle, a square, and a regular pentagon on cardboard, and cut them out. Then you can make each figure by tracing around the cardboard form.

There are only five regular solids. The tetrahedron has four faces, each a triangle. The octahedron is an eight-faced regular solid.

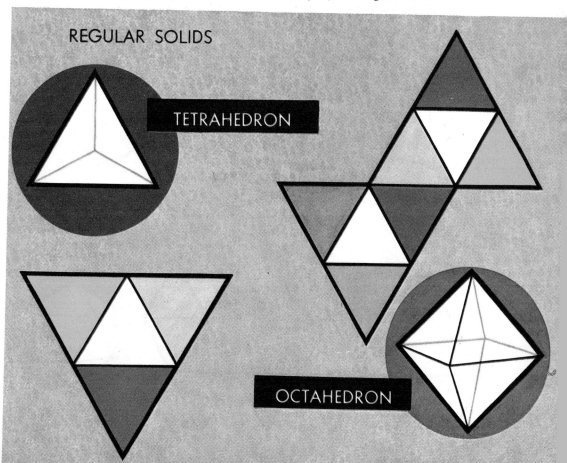

REGULAR SOLIDS

TETRAHEDRON

OCTAHEDRON

REGULAR SOLIDS

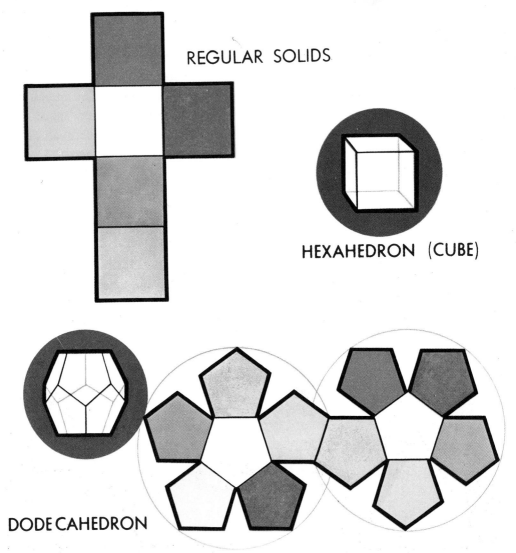

HEXAHEDRON (CUBE)

DODECAHEDRON

You can make a dodecahedron by tracing the patterns above. Transfer your tracing onto cardboard and cut around the edges, on the heavy black lines. Crease along the lines, and fasten the edges together with adhesive tape. To make an icosahedron, follow the same steps after tracing the pattern below.

ICOSAHEDRON

Mathematics
in Nature

In nature we can see some beautiful examples of the curves and polygons and solids that are studied in mathematics.

At the top of this page we see a snowflake. All snowflakes are built around the same form, the regular hexagon. Next to the snowflake we see the hexagon again, in a honeycomb built by bees.

Beneath the honeycomb is a shell of the nautilus, an animal that lives in the sea. It has been cut open to show the chambers inside. The curve that winds out from the center is called a spiral. At the bottom of the page we see many spirals like it, winding out in two directions from the center of the giant sunflower.

29

When volcanoes are formed, the hot lava often spills out in the shape of a cone. In the sky above, the moon, the sun, and the stars are all spheres. We can see the spherical shape clearly in the moon, which is the nearest body in our solar system to the earth.

The pictures at the left show the skeletons of some radiolarians. They are tiny animals that live in the sea. The floors of the Pacific and Indian Oceans are covered with such skeletons, left by animals that lived millions of years ago. Each is a perfectly symmetrical polygon. The skeleton at the top of the panel is an almost perfect octahedron, or eight-faced solid figure. The second one is a dodecahedron, with twelve faces. The third is an icosahedron, or twenty-faced solid figure.

Letters for Numbers

We know that $1 + 2 = 2 + 1$, $2 + 3 = 3 + 2$, $4 + 7 = 7 + 4$. We can make any number of true statements like this. Simply write a first number plus a second number on one side of the equals sign. On the other side, let the numbers change places.

Instead of writing each statement separately, we can write them all at once in this way. Let the letter a stand for any number. Let the letter b stand for any other number. Then we simply write: $a + b = b + a$. When we do this, we have taken the step from arithmetic to *algebra*.

In algebra, we let letters stand for numbers. It is like using a code for say-ing many things in a small space. In this code, we do not use $\times$ to mean "times," because we may mix it up with the letter x. We show multiplication by using a dot instead, or by writing the multipliers side by side with no symbol between them. In this code, $a \cdot b$ means, "the number that a stands for, multiplied by the number that b stands for." It is usually written ab.

When the same mutiplier is used over and over again, we use the same way of writing the product that we used for square and cubic numbers on pages 13 to 15. When we write x^4, called x to the fourth power, we mean $x \cdot x \cdot x \cdot x$, or x used as a multiplier 4 times.

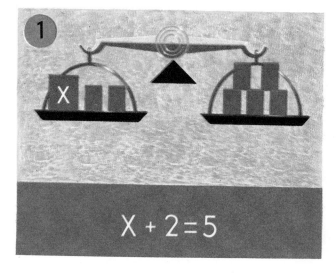

Algebraic equations work the way scales do. Whatever you put on one side of the equation or the scales must be equal to the number or weight on the other side, in order to balance.

Here is a statement in code that is not always true: $x + 2 = 5$. It is not true if x stands for 7, because $7 + 2$ is not 5. It is true if x stands for 3. A statement like this is called an *equation*. To solve the equation means to find the number which makes it true.

An equation resembles a balance scale. The $x + 2$ is supposed to balance the 5 the way equal weights balance on a scale. If we change one weight on a scale, we can make the weights balance again by changing the other weight in the same way. This is a hint on how we can solve an equation: simply change both sides of the equation in the same way, by adding or subtracting, or by multiplying or dividing. Since 5 is the same as $3 + 2$, the equation $x + 2 = 5$ says: $x + 2 = 3 + 2$. If we take away 2 from both sides, they will still balance each other. In this way we find that $x = 3$ is the answer. To

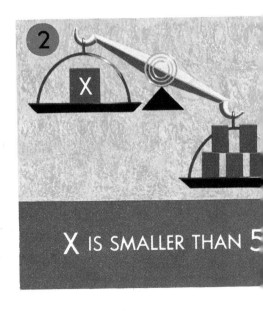

X IS SMALLER THAN 5

solve the equation $3x = 12$, we divide both sides by 3, and we get $x = 4$ as the answer to the problem.

Can you solve the equation $3x - 4 = 8$? To find the answer, add 4 to each side of the equation, and then divide each side by 3.

The word *algebra* has a thousand-year history. It comes from the title of a book about equations written by the Arabian mathematician, al-Khowarizmi. The book was called *al-jabr w'al-muqa-balah*. These words describe the method of solving an equation by adding or subtracting the same number on both sides. When the book was translated into Latin, the title became *Ludus algebrae almucgrabalaeque*. About four hundred years ago it was written in English as *algiebar and almachabel*. Then it was shortened to the single word *algebra*.

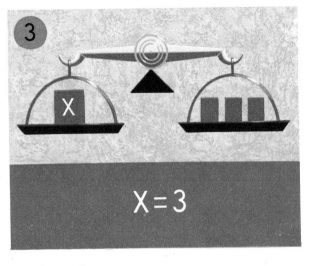

X = 3

Navigation

A navigator has two kinds of problems to solve. One is to find out where he is on the earth, at any moment. The other is to figure out what course his ship should take to go from one place to another. His tools for solving these problems are a compass, a sextant, a clock, and an almanac. His compass tells him which way is north, so he can measure directions correctly. With his sextant he can measure the height of the sun, moon, or a star above the horizon. His clock tells him what time it is in Greenwich, England. And his almanac tells him how the sky looks at Greenwich any day of the year and any time of the day. When he has all this information, he can figure out the answer to his problem.

Let us see how he can locate his position on the earth. The earth is a sphere spinning on its axis. The axis points almost directly to Polaris, the North Star. The diagram below, right, shows men in different positions on the earth looking at Polaris. The man on the equator sees Polaris lying directly on his horizon.

For the others, a line to Polaris makes an angle with the horizon. The further

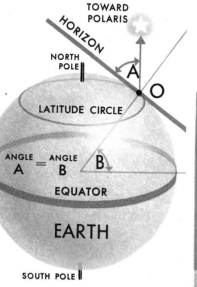

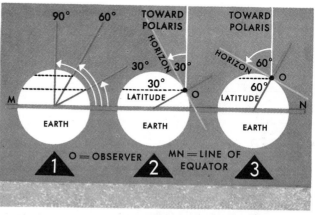

At the equator, a man would see Polaris, the North Star, right on the horizon. As he moved north, he would see Polaris making an angle with the horizon. By measuring this angle, he can tell how far north he is from the equator.

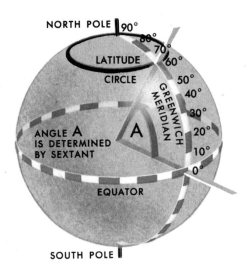

NORTH POLE 90°
80°
70°
LATITUDE 60°
CIRCLE 50°
40°
GREENWICH MERIDIAN
30°
ANGLE A 20°
IS DETERMINED A 10°
BY SEXTANT 0°
EQUATOR

SOUTH POLE

land, where a naval observatory is located. His clock tells him the time at Greenwich. His almanac tells him what the sky looks like there.

The position of the stars in the sky above him looks different. Compared to the sky as seen from Greenwich, it looks as though it were turned through an angle. The amount of this turning tells him how far around the earth he is from the place where the meridian

north the man is, the larger the angle is. So, measuring this angle tells him how far north he is above the equator. If the angle is 30 degrees, then he knows he is somewhere on the latitude circle 30 degrees above the equator. Now he has to find out where he is on that circle.

This circle is crossed by the meridian that passes through Greenwich, Eng-

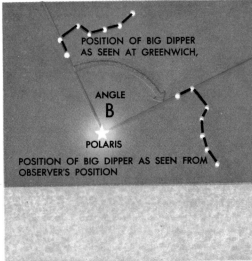

POSITION OF BIG DIPPER AS SEEN AT GREENWICH,

ANGLE
B

POLARIS
POSITION OF BIG DIPPER AS SEEN FROM OBSERVER'S POSITION

through Greenwich crosses his latitude circle. This information fixes his position. Then he can look at a naval chart, (which is just a map of the oceans with latitude circles and meridians marked on it), and find out exactly where he is.

Using a clock and an almanac, a man who knows how far from the equator he is, can also tell how far east or west he is from the Greenwich meridian. Thus, he can find his exact position on the earth.

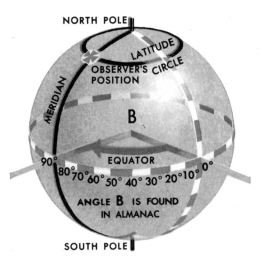

NORTH POLE

LATITUDE
OBSERVER'S CIRCLE
POSITION
MERIDIAN
B

90° EQUATOR 0°
80° 70° 60° 50° 40° 30° 20° 10°

ANGLE B IS FOUND
IN ALMANAC

SOUTH POLE

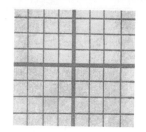

Your Number in Space

Many big cities are divided into blocks by streets running in one direction, and avenues crossing them at right angles. You can locate any street corner by mentioning two numbers: the number of the street and the number of the avenue that crosses it. Thus, if you wanted to meet a friend in New York City, you might say, "I'll meet you near the Public Library, at Fifth Avenue and Forty-second Street."

In the same way, we can locate any seat in a classroom by calling out two numbers: the row number and the seat number. In the picture, the rows are numbered from left to right, and the seats from the front to back. The teacher has just said, "Raise your hand if your row number and seat number add up to 5." The locations of the pupils who raised their hands are given by the pairs of numbers, (4,1), (3,2), (2,3), and (1,4), where the first number in each pair is the row number. If we let r stand for row number, and s stand for seat number, we can describe these locations by means of the equation: $r + s = 5$. Notice that the pupils whose hands are up are arranged in a straight line. The equation is a description of the locations on this line. Also the line is a picture of the pairs of numbers described by the equation.

This is an example of an important discovery made three hundred years ago by the French mathematician, René Descartes. An equation with two unknown numbers can be pictured by means of a line (straight or curved), called a *graph*. Also, every line is described by means of an equation. The

1597854

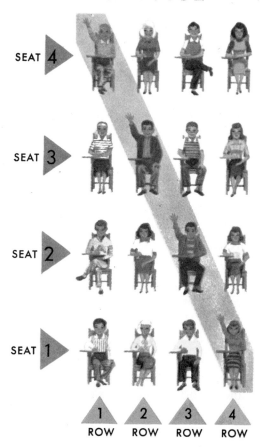

35

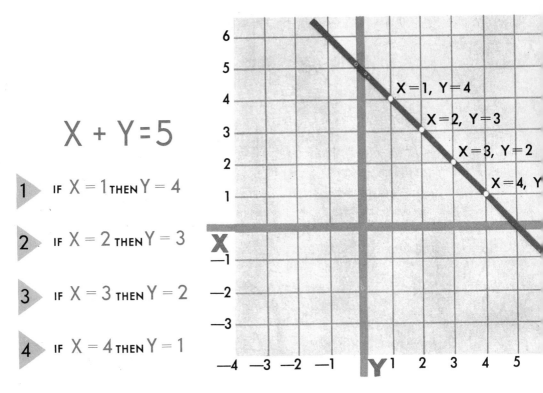

$$X + Y = 5$$

1 ▸ IF $X = 1$ THEN $Y = 4$

2 ▸ IF $X = 2$ THEN $Y = 3$

3 ▸ IF $X = 3$ THEN $Y = 2$

4 ▸ IF $X = 4$ THEN $Y = 1$

Rene Descartes, a French mathematician, discovered that an equation with two unknown numbers can be shown by means of a graph, on which every line is an equation.

branch of mathematics that grew out of this discovery is called *analytic geometry*.

The connection between a line and its equation is usually shown in this way: on a sheet of graph paper, we pick out one horizontal line and one vertical line and call each the zero line or axis. Then we number the other lines by counting lines away from each axis, in both directions. In one direction we attach a plus sign to each number. In the opposite direction, we use a minus sign, so we can tell them apart. Then each intersection is described by a pair

of numbers, telling you how far it is right or left and up or down from the axes. We call the right or left number the *x* number. The up or down number is the *y* number. Numbers with fractions describe points that are between the lines.

Here are some examples of equations whose graphs are curved lines: The graph of $x^2 + y^2 = 25$ is a *circle*. The graph of $4x^2 + 9y^2 = 25$ is an oval-shaped curve called an *ellipse*. The graph of $y = 4x - x^2$ is a *parabola*. It is shaped like the path followed by a baseball when the batter hits a "fly."

Heads or Tails?

Figuring out the chance that something will happen is like looking into the future. It is done by using common sense and a knowledge of what happened in the past. To see how it works in a simple case, let us try to foresee what happens when you toss a coin. The coin has two faces, head and tail, and each is as likely to come up as the other. Common sense and experience join to tell us that, out of a large number of tosses, about half will come out heads, and the rest will be tails. Saying it another way: on the average, one out of two tosses will come out heads. So the chance of getting a head is ½.

If we toss two coins, there are three possible results. We may get two heads, or two tails, or one head and one tail. What is the chance of getting each of these results? It is *not* one out of three. If we use two different coins (say a penny and a dime), we see that there are really four possible results. Throwing the penny first and the dime second, we might get head-head, or head-tail, or tail-head, or tail-tail. The chance of getting two heads is one out of four, or ¼. The chance of getting two tails is also ¼. The chance of getting one head and one tail is two out of four tosses, or ½.

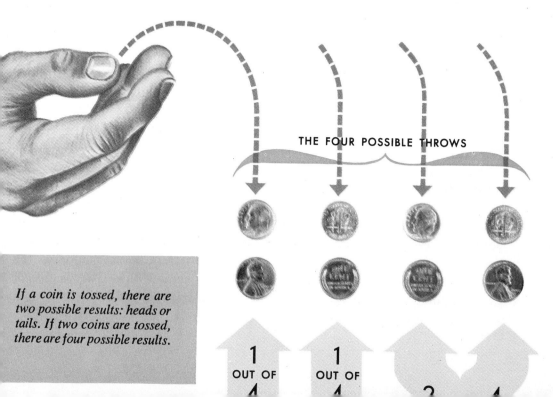

THE FOUR POSSIBLE THROWS

If a coin is tossed, there are two possible results: heads or tails. If two coins are tossed, there are four possible results.

1 OUT OF 4   1 OUT OF 4   2   4

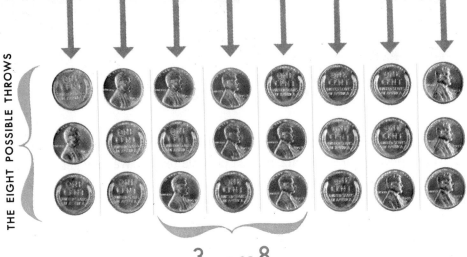

3 OUT OF 8

What is the chance of getting two heads and a tail when you toss three coins? To answer this question, we must first notice that there are three ways of getting two heads and a tail. We may get head-head-tail, or head-tail-head, or tail-head-head. Then we must compare this number with the total number of ways three coins can fall. This number is eight, because each coin can fall in two ways, and $2 \times 2 \times 2 = 8$. So the chance of getting two heads and a tail is ⅜.

There is a shortcut for finding the chance of getting any special combination. This is *Pascal's triangle*. Pascal, a French philosopher and mathematician of the 17th century, was for a time interested in roulette and other games of chance. This interest led him to discover certain important rules about the possibilities of getting heads or tails on the toss of a coin. His findings are described in a triangular formation of numbers, which shows easily the pos-

sibility of getting heads or tails, or any combination of them, on a given number of tosses of a coin.

Each line in the triangle is obtained from the line above it in this way. Write a 1 at each end of every line; then, under each pair of numbers that are side by side, write their sum. The first line tells the chances of getting head or tails in tossing one coin; the second line, with two coins; the third line with three coins, and so on. The first number in a line shows the chances of getting all heads. The next number in each line is the chance for getting all but one head, and one tail, and so on down the line. To figure the probabilities for tossing four coins, use the fourth line. For the chances of getting two heads and two tails with four coins, use the third number in that line. Compare this number to the sum of all the numbers in that line. The chance of getting two heads and two tails is 6 out of 16, or ⅜.

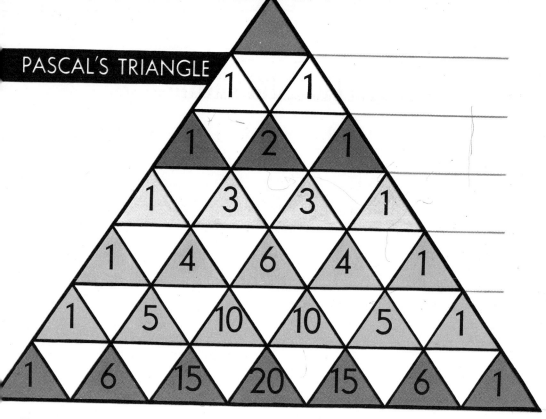

PASCAL'S TRIANGLE

1 COIN		*If you toss one coin, the chance of having it land with the head emblem up will be 1 out of 2, or ½.*
2 COINS		*If you toss two coins, your chance of getting 2 heads is 1 out of 4; of getting 1 head and 1 tail, 2 out of 4 or ½; of getting 2 tails, 1 out of 4.*
3 COINS		*If you toss three coins, your chances are: all heads, 1 out of 8; 2 heads and 1 tail, 3 out of 8; 2 tails and 1 head, 3 out of 8; all tails, 1 out of 8.*
4 COINS		*If four coins are tossed, there is 1 chance in 16 of getting all heads or all tails; 4 out of 16 of getting 3 heads, 1 tail, or 3 tails and 1 head; 6 out of 16 of getting 2 heads and 2 tails.*
5 COINS		*In five tosses, chances are: 1 out of 32 for all heads or all tails; 5 out of 32 for 4 heads, 1 tail or 4 tails, 1 head; 10 out of 32 for 3 heads, 2 tails or 3 tails and 2 heads.*
6 COINS		*In six tosses, the chances for all heads or all tails are 1 in 64; for 5 heads and 1 tail, or the reverse, 6 out of 64; 4 heads and 2 tails (or reverse), 15 out of 64; 3 and 3, 20 out of 64.*

39

The Slide Rule—
The Stick That Multiplies

When we solve a problem, we try to figure it out in the shortest and easiest way. The easiest way to solve a problem is not to work on it at all. Let a machine do it for you, instead.

You can make your own adding machine out of two ordinary rulers. Simply place one ruler next to the other, edge to edge. Now your machine is ready for use. If you want to add 2 and 3, place the zero-edge of the upper ruler over the 2 on the lower ruler. Then locate the 3 on the upper ruler. Use the line that belongs to the 3 as a pointer. It points out the answer on the lower ruler.

By making a slight change in the rulers, we can turn them into a machine that multiplies. We get a hint on how to do it from one of the things we learned on page 15.

A short way of writing $2 \cdot 2 \cdot 2 \cdot 2$ is 2^4. But $2 \cdot 2 \cdot 2 \cdot 2 = 16$. So 2^4 is another way of writing 16. The 4, which tells us how many 2's to multiply to get 16, is called the *logarithm* of 16. In the same way, 2^3 is another way of writing 8, and the logarithm of 8 is 3. To mul-

A pair of ordinary foot rulers can be used to add numbers together.

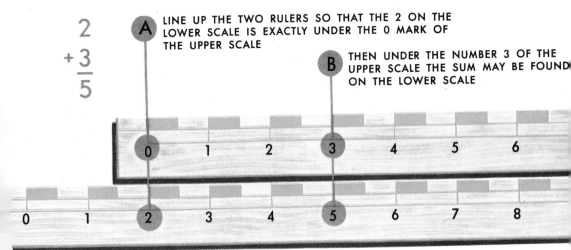

$$\begin{array}{r} 2 \\ +3 \\ \hline 5 \end{array}$$

A LINE UP THE TWO RULERS SO THAT THE 2 ON THE LOWER SCALE IS EXACTLY UNDER THE 0 MARK OF THE UPPER SCALE

B THEN UNDER THE NUMBER 3 OF THE UPPER SCALE THE SUM MAY BE FOUND ON THE LOWER SCALE

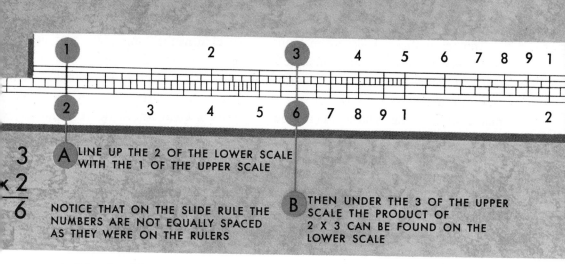

A slide rule adds logarithms in order to do multiplication problems simply.

tiply 16 by 8, we multiply 2^4 by 2^3. That means take $2 \cdot 2 \cdot 2 \cdot 2$ times $2 \cdot 2 \cdot 2$. Replacing the word "times" by a multiplication sign, we get $2 \cdot 2 \cdot 2 \cdot 2 \cdot 2 \cdot 2 \cdot 2$. The short way of writing this result is 2^7. This number, multiplied out is 128, and its logarithm is 7.

Notice that while the numbers 16 and 8 were multiplied to get 128, their logarithms, 4 and 3, were *added* to get 7. This is our hint. We know already that two rulers can add the distances that are measured on them. So we make up a special pair of rulers in which the distance of each number from the end of the ruler is equal to the logarithm of the number. The rulers will add the logarithms. But adding the logarithms is like multiplying the numbers. These special rulers are called a *slide rule*.

Two ordinary foot rulers can subtract numbers as well as add them. For example, to subtract 3 from 5, place the 3 of the upper ruler over the 5 of the lower ruler. Then the 0 of the upper ruler points out the answer, 2. In the same way, a slide rule that multiplies numbers can be used backwards to divide numbers.

Slide rules are used by people in many different kinds of work—engineers, architects, printers, and anyone else who has to make many rapid calculations. There are many kinds of slide rules. Besides the straight slide rules described above, there are circular slide rules. They are printed on two circular cards of different sizes. The cards are mounted center over center like two wheels on the same axle, and are free to turn.

41

Counting Wheels

Another simple calculating machine is the *odometer* in a car, which tells you how many miles the car has traveled. It is made up of a series of wheels placed side by side. The numbers from 0 to 9 are printed on the rim of each wheel. One of these numbers on each wheel shows through the little window on the dashboard. The wheel on the right counts tenths of a mile. When the car travels one tenth of a mile, the wheel turns around just enough to move the next higher number into place at the window. After 9 tenths of a mile, the number 9 shows through the window. After the next tenth, the wheel turns the 0 into place, and, at the same time turns the wheel next to it one space. The effect is to exchange ten spaces on the first wheel for one space on the second wheel. In the same way the second wheel, after completing a full turn, exchanges ten spaces for one space on the third wheel. So, while the first wheel counts tenths of a mile, the second wheel counts whole miles, the third wheel counts tens of miles, the fourth wheel counts hundreds of miles, and so on. Most desk calculators work in the same way. They are simply counting machines. They add two numbers the way people add on their fin-

Automobiles have a small measuring machine on the dashboard, called an odometer, which measures the distance that the car travels and produces the numbers on a moving dial.

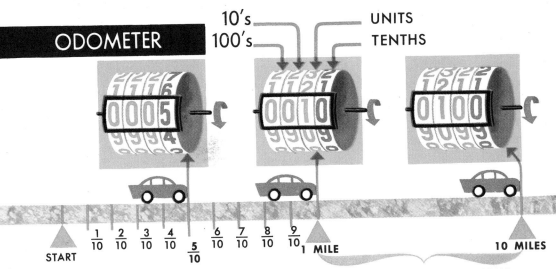

THIS DISTANCE IS NOT IN SCALE

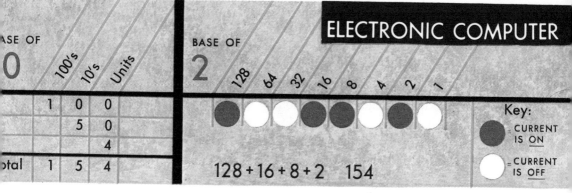

ASE OF 0	100's	10's	Units
	1	0	0
		5	0
			4
otal	1	5	4

BASE OF 2 — 128 64 32 16 8 4 2 1

128 + 16 + 8 + 2 = 154

Key:
= CURRENT IS ON
= CURRENT IS OFF

Electronic computers work by adding 2 figures together very rapidly. They turn the current on and off in a series of electrical circuits, building up large numbers in groups of two.

gers. They count out the first number, and then, starting where the first number leaves off, they count out the second number. They multiply by adding the same number many times. To multiply 4 × 5, for example, a desk calculator adds 5, 5, 5, and 5.

The fastest calculators are the machines that work electronically. They are counting machines. Instead of having a series of turning wheels, they use a series of electrical circuits. They keep count by turning currents on and off in these circuits. Just as in the odometer, one wheel passes the count on to the next by turning it, in electronic calculators one circuit passes the count on to the next circuit by turning its current on or off.

Each wheel in an odometer has ten positions, so the odometer builds up large numbers in groups of ten. Each circuit in an electronic calculator has just two positions, on and off. So an electronic calculator builds up large numbers in groups of two. Although this is a slower way of counting, electronic calculators work very rapidly, because electric currents travel almost as fast as light.

Machines that build up large numbers in groups of two, write numbers in a special way. In ordinary numerals, the 1 of 10 means one group of *ten.* When these machines write numbers, the 1 of 10 means one group of *two.* In their system of writing, known as the *binary scale,* 10 means *two,* 11 means *three,* and 100 stands for *four.*

The odometer, desk calculator, and counting machine are all called *digital machines,* as they count numbers or digits. There is another type of calculator which measures instead of counts. These machines can combine and measure such quantities as length, angle, and electric current. The slide rule is one kind of non-digital calculator.

43

Mathematics and Music

A musical tone is made by vibration. For example, if we stretch a string tightly and then pluck it, it will vibrate and produce a tone. What the tone sounds like depends on the number of vibrations that the string makes. The number of vibrations per second is called the frequency of the tone, or the pitch. When a song is written, it is always composed of a family of tones called a *key*. To see how the tones in a key are related, let us actually build one.

The most important tone in a key is the one on which the song ends. It is called the *tonic*. Let us choose as a tonic the tone made by a string that

The tone made by a violin string depends on the number of times the string vibrates.

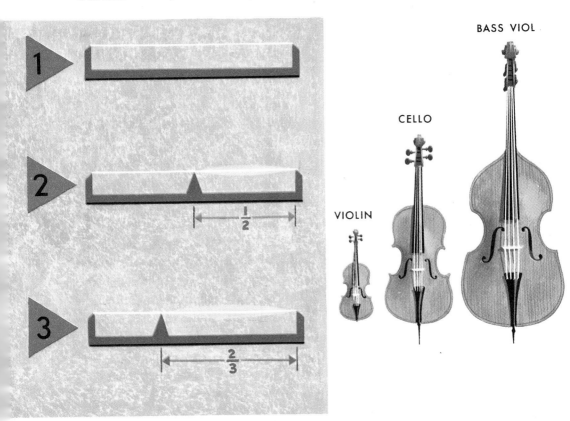

vibrates 256 times a second. We call this tone C. If we cut the string in half, it will vibrate twice as fast. The tone made by this shorter string is also called C. Its frequency is 512 vibrations per second. The frequency 256 is double 128, and this is double 64, and so on. We call all these tones C because we think of them as the same sound at different levels.

Now let us vibrate a string whose length is ⅔ the length of the original one. The tone it produces is the tonic's closest relative. We call it the *dominant*. Its frequency is $\frac{3}{2}$ times as great as the frequency of the tonic. *A key is a family of tones in which each tone is the dominant of some other tone in the group.* To find the dominant of any tone in the family, we multiply its frequency by $\frac{3}{2}$ or 1½.

By multiplying over and over again by $\frac{3}{2}$ we get a chain of tones each of which is the dominant of the one before it. These tones are called G, D, A, E, and B. Dividing 256 by $\frac{3}{2}$, we get 171, the frequency of the tone F, for which C is the dominant. These tones make up the key of C.

We started with the tone C that has a frequency of 256. The next higher C has a frequency of 512. We can get all of the tones of our key to lie between these limits, for when the frequency of a tone is too high, we can divide it in half, and still have the same tone but at a lower frequency. Our G is not too high, so we keep it. All the others ex-

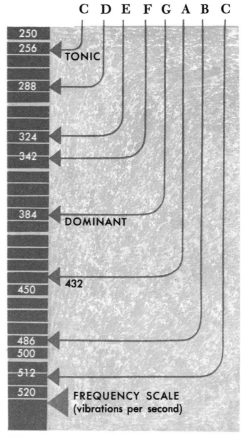

We can produce the same sound at different levels by halving or doubling the length of the instrument's string.

cept F are too high, so we divide by 2 over and over again until the frequency lies between 256 and 512. The frequency of F is too low, so we double it. Now, arranged in order of frequency, we have a ladder of tones called a *scale* from C to the next higher C. C (256), D (288), E (324), F (342), G (384), A (432), B (486), C (512). This is the order of the white keys on a piano keyboard.

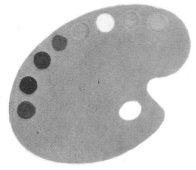

Mathematics and Art

An Egyptian painting drawn without using perspective.

Compare the two pictures that are on this page. The one at the top is an Egyptian painting. The human figures in it all look flat. You cannot tell which ones are meant to be nearer to you. The other picture is a painting by the Italian artist, de Chirico. The buildings in the picture look solid. You can see that some are higher than others and are further away. You can see also that there is a large courtyard that stretches far away from you into the distance. The space in de Chirico's painting looks more real than that of the Egyptian painting because he used mathematics when he laid it out on his canvas.

In this painting, "Delights of the Poet," de Chirico has used perspective to create a feeling of depth and distance.

The great German artist, Albrecht Dürer, said, "Geometry is the right foundation of painting." To make a painting look real, the painter thinks of his canvas as a "window" through which he is looking at a scene that is behind it. He reasons in this way: each point of the scene sends a ray of light to the eye of the person looking at it. These rays of light pass through the "window" between the eye and the scene. The place where a ray crosses the window is the place where the point it comes from will appear in the picture. The collection of rays going from the scene to the eye is called a *projection*. The picture formed where the window crosses the projection is called a *section*. To figure out what the section will look like is a problem in *perspective*. The rules of perspective were worked out with the help of geometry.

In de Chirico's painting you see how he used two of the rules of perspective: the further away something is, the smaller it looks; and parallel lines that go off into the distance, like straight railroad tracks, look as though they come to a point.

There are many bridges connecting mathematics and art. Here is how the Fibonacci fractions (p. 17) serve as a bridge. Not all rectangles are equally pleasing to the eye. There is a best-looking shape for rectangles in which the ratio of the width to the length is called the *golden mean*. The Fibonacci fractions are close to this ratio. The further out a fraction is in the series, the closer it is to the golden mean.

Mathematics helped art through the science of perspective. But then art repaid its debt. The study of perspective led to the development of a new branch of mathematics which was called *projective geometry*.

Parallel lines appear to come together to a point as they recede from the observer.

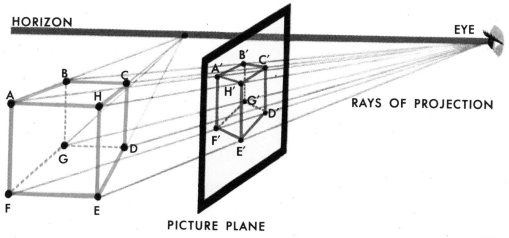

The Number on the Card

Many card tricks are worked mathematically. This one is easy, but looks very mysterious.

Use a deck of 52 cards and shuffle it well. Ask someone in your audience to count out three stacks of cards from the full deck, while you turn your back

so you cannot see the cards. He should follow these directions:

Put the first card face up, and start counting with the number on the card. Think of an Ace as 1, Jack as 11, Queen as 12, and King as 13. Count out more cards on top of the first one

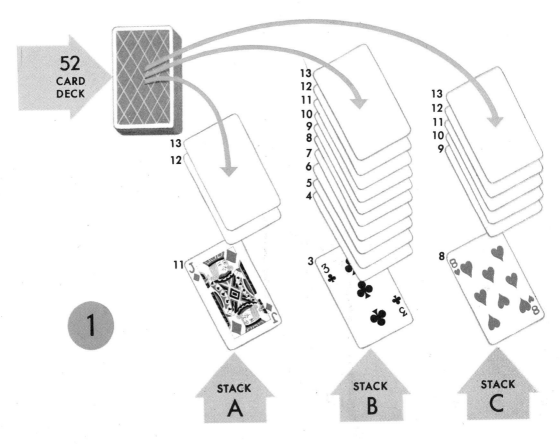

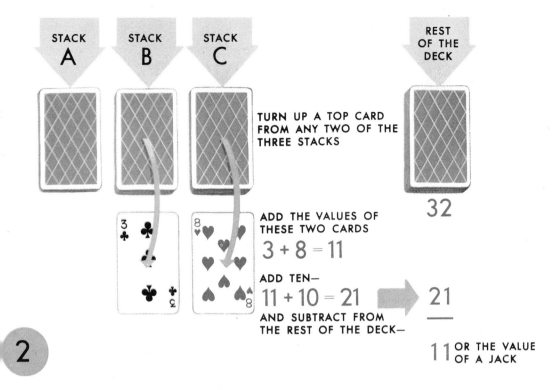

STACK **A**　STACK **B**　STACK **C**

REST OF THE DECK

TURN UP A TOP CARD FROM ANY TWO OF THE THREE STACKS

ADD THE VALUES OF THESE TWO CARDS

$3 + 8 = 11$

ADD TEN—

$11 + 10 = 21$ ➡ 21

AND SUBTRACT FROM THE REST OF THE DECK—

32

2

11 OR THE VALUE OF A JACK

Many card tricks can be worked out mathematically. In the one described here, jacks, queens, and kings have the value of 11, 12, and 13, and aces have the value of 1.

until you reach 13. If the first card is a 6, for example, you will say as you count out more cards: 7, 8, 9, 10, 11, 12, 13. You will reach 13 when you have put seven more cards on top of the first one. If the first card is a King, which already has the value of 13, you won't have to put any more cards on top of it. Turn the stack over and start a new stack, counting again up to 13. Do it once more, so that there are three stacks on the table, *face down*. Now ask for the cards that are left over. Count them, and remember the number. Ask someone in the audience to

turn up the top card in any two of the stacks. Then you tell them, without looking at it, what the top card on the other stack is.

You figure it out this way: add the numbers of the two cards turned up, and add ten to the result. Then subtract the sum from the number you got by counting the left-over cards. For example, if the cards turned up are 3 and 8, and the number of left-over cards is 32, you add 3 + 8 + 10, giving you 21. When you subtract 21 from 32, you get 11. So you know that the top card of the third stack is a Jack.

Q.E.D.

Proving It

Many statements may be made about numbers or space. Some of the statements are true, and some are false. Mathematics has the job of finding out which ones are true, and proving that they are true. This is done by always following the rules of *logic*, or the science of correct reasoning.

ber x stands for if the equation is a true statement.

The equation says that the number which $3x + 5$ stands for, and the number 20, are equal. This is the first link in the chain. We join it to the second link with the help of a rule that we know is true. This rule says that if we

$$3X + 5 = 20$$

One type of proof often used in mathematics is a kind of *chain reasoning*. In this type of proof we move forward towards our result through a series of steps, each of which leads to the next, like links in a chain. We use this kind of reasoning, for example, when we solve an equation like: $3x + 5 = 20$. Our problem is to find out what num-

subtract the same number from equal numbers, we get equal results. So we subtract 5 from both numbers, and get the equation $3x = 15$. This is the second link in the chain. We join it to the third link by using another rule that we know is true. This rule says that if we divide equal numbers by the same number, we get equal results. So we divide

$$3X + 5 = 20 \qquad \begin{array}{c} (3X+5)-5=20-5 \\ 3X = 15 \end{array}$$

by 3, and get the equation $x = 5$. This is the third link in the chain. The three-link chain tells us then, that if $3x + 5 = 20$, then x must equal 5.

There is another kind of proof in which we back into our result instead of moving forward to it. We use a process of *elimination*. We first list a series of statements, chosen so that we are sure that one of them must be true. Next, we eliminate all the statements except one by proving they are false. Then the statement that is left must be the one that is true.

it means that there are more than twelve different months. This is impossible, because there are only twelve months. So we must eliminate statement (2). Then we are sure that statement (1) must be true, because it is the only one left.

There is a third type of proof in which a theory is checked in two steps. First the laws of probability are used to draw conclusions from the theory. Then the conclusions are compared with the results of a series of experiments. We find out the *probability* that the theory is true by seeing how well the results match the con-

$$3X + 5 = 20 \qquad 3X = 15 \qquad \begin{array}{c} 3X \div 3 = 15 \div 3 \\ X = 5 \end{array}$$

Here is an example of reasoning by elimination. Suppose there are *more than* twelve people in a room. Then we shall prove that at least two of them have their birthdays in the same month. First we list two statements: (1) at least two of the people in the room have birthdays in the same month. (2) no two of the people in the room have birthdays in the same month. We are sure one of these statements must be true. Now, if statement (2) is true, it means that the people in the room all have birthdays in *different* months. But, if there are more than twelve people in the room, and their birthdays are in different months,

clusions. Suppose, for example, a gambler bets that when he tosses five coins, they will turn up five heads. Let the theory be that the tossing is honest. The conclusion from the theory is that five heads will turn up only about once out of every 32 tosses. (See p. 38). Now we watch the gambler toss the coins. Each toss is an experiment. Suppose he tosses the coins 300 times, and they turn up all heads 150 times. Then the results of the experiments do not match the conclusions from the theory. We would then conclude that the theory is *probably* false. The laws of probability suggest that the tossing is not honest.

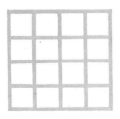

Magic Squares

The arrangement of numbers shown below is called a five-by-five magic square. It uses all the whole numbers from 1 to 25. If you add the numbers in any row, or any column, or either diagonal, you always get the same sum.

Use the numbers from 1 to 9 to make a three-by-three magic square. Properly placed, the rows, columns, and diagonals will add up to the same sum.

Adding *all* the numbers from 1 to 9 is like finding the 9th triangle number. Using the rule given on page 13, we multiply 9 by 10, and then divide by 2. The result is 45. This will be the sum of all the numbers. Since they are spread out in three rows, we find what the sum of one row should be by dividing 45, the sum of all the rows, by 3. So each row should add up to 15.

17	24	1	8	15
23	5	7	14	16
4	6	13	20	22
10	12	19	21	3
11	18	25	2	9

Mathematics in Use Today

Mathematics is part of our daily lives. A housekeeper uses mathematics when she goes shopping. She compares prices, figures out her bills, and counts her change.

A bookkeeper uses mathematics to keep track of a company's income and expenses.

A machinist uses mathematics when he plans his work. He must measure and figure to know how to set his tool, so that it will cut out parts with the right size and shape.

The navigator on an airplane uses mathematics to help him chart his course. He must figure distances and directions to know how to get from Hawaii to Tokyo.

An astronomer uses mathematics to figure out how far away the stars are. He uses equations to help explain how stars are formed, what makes them shine, and how they change as they grow older.

The physicist uses mathematics to explore the mysteries of the atom. His experiments give him facts. His equations show how these facts are related, and often lead to new facts that were never known before.

And so, in many different ways, mathematics has shaped civilization as we know it today.

Index

Picture on p. 46 courtesy the Museum of Modern Art

D